MW01247399

FIND YOUR FIRE

A Poem Book

KAREEM GALATHE

FIND YOUR FIRE

Finding your fire is when you are at your highest capacity. It is when your insides are warm, and your mind is completely blown away by what you've just experienced. It makes you do things that you have only thought about. Have you ever experienced this?

All you have to do is stop denying yourself what it is that you want. Find and receive all it has to offer. As your mind starts to drift and your body starts to sweat, you feel as though you are moving to the melodies of a flute. Then you realize that you are not sweating it is just love's tongue moving across every inch of your person. Does this make you think of what you've denied your self of? I have experienced this. I will continue to experience this, what about you?

FALLEN

I saw this queen in my dreams

I think I've fallen

I feel this queen

I think I've fallen

When this queen speaks her tone of voice is very soothing, like profound poetry is being read to me

I think I've fallen

When she touches me, its like her hand is sculpting every curve of my body

I think I've fallen

When she looks at me, it is like she's drowning me in her deep brown eyes

I think I've fallen

I can sense when she is near, almost like I can smell her

When she isn't close, it feels as if she is like a drug that my soul craves

There is no detox healthy enough for that

I think I've fallen

To hear her voice is like a soothing blanket that keeps my wrapped uptight

She calls me spoiled, and she'd like to keep me that way

She's a queen strong enough to be king

I have fallen

She has kept me like a king, magnificent to look at, yet fragile to touch

I think that is why she tries to keep me all to herself

I like that because that lets me know that she too has fallen

in LOVE

HER

He lets her be her

He excepts her for her

When he looks at her

He sees the inner side of her being

She doesn't need to have

long hair or big breasts

He says that her body is just beautiful, and she should believe in
that

He's happy with just her

He excepts her for her

Her beauty is not a question here

What's at issue here is the beauty

He has to have beauty, not to question hers.

IMAGINE

Imagine holding hands and walking in the park

Imagine kissing someone you that you are so in love with

Imagine a long drive with your favorite songs

Imagine lavender skies, yellow trees and

a 60-degree fall breeze

Imagine sand, wind, green water and your best friend

Imagine Love at first sight

Imagine a canoe in secluded waters

Imagine seeing more than the physical.

Imagine being truly in Love and Happy.

DISTANCE

Also though you vowed to come back, the point is I'm missing you

Is it someone else?

Is it that I've changed so much that I've outgrown you?

Or is it that you've outgrown me?

When I cry it's because I'm missing you

Us without each other is like a beautiful day with no sun, what's the use?

My heart hurts, and you ask why? as if you care

When I cry in front of you, you stand there and stare

Am I missing you SOB don't you even care?

Even though you left on bad terms, vowed to come back,

I might not want your ass, so stay where you're at!

THE RAIN

Explaining raindrops would be like comparing them to angel fingerprints. You might feel them, but you don't see them..

You can do anything in the rain because it covers up a lot.

You can even cry in the rain since you are already wet; no one can see your tears.

Sometimes I cry, and there is no rain, and it's a shame that sometimes there's no rain to camouflage my pain…

When you are in pain or love, the rain can be used as an excuse for how you are feeling.

You see, you can make love in the rain, or be in pain because you can't make love.

BLISSFUL COMMUTE

My thoughts wander to different places throughout my day. Views to such sites of Paris to the Atlantic, the Atlantic to California.

I genuinely feel that my mind wanders because I'm trying not to think of what is really in front of me.

I see things like day to day drugs that come so close to home it is unbelievable,

I see things ending that should have never stopped.

I pray for help in dealing with these situations.

Even though I know within it is not going to help me because

I have trouble believing in what it is that I am praying for.

So that is why my mind wanders to such places like Spain to the Pacific, from the Pacific to Brazil. Some of these places I may never visit, I strongly feel that if my faith is strong, my limit is the sky. Are your views on life a Mindful?

WHEN WAS THE LAST TIME

When was the last time you cried after lovemaking so intense you broke into a cold sweat?

When was the last time the aches and pains of your body were licked away?

When was the last time you had a body massage that turned into toe sucking?

Man, if you have never experienced this, what is your sex life like?

To me, it is about two people feeling each other inside and out. Two people are becoming one flesh, one sweat.

When was the last time your brain was mentally stimulated with an in-depth conversation?

A conversation that had you longing to be near this person to hear what they will say next.

When was the last time you had sexual stimulation with just eye contact?

You can't do this with someone you don't know. This has to be someone whom you've known in a previous lifetime.

Someone who knows you like the back of your hand.

When you come across this person, you'll feel it the instant stimulation!

DEATH OF THE EGO

When a man cries sometimes, you can hear it a mile away

A man's cry is almost like a loud piercing sound

There are so many reasons for why a man cries

To all the men not feeling how they should, keep your head up,

there's always light at the end of your dark tunnel

Don't cry sir; there is love in you to love your self

Sometimes this world can seem like a joke

The only thing you can do is get consumed by this strange world, or wake up and do something about how your life may turn out you only are able

if you are strong

Look past all the fake Money, Power, and Respect

You only get that if you earn it

Obey your thirst

Don't obey the thirst of drugs and sex

Do; follow your desire to know about God and what it is that he and she can do for you

You have to believe that you have the knowledge and wisdom to make a place for your self in a world that is good to you when you are kind to it

Don't pollute your soul with self-hate

Believe in God before it is too late

If there is stress on your chess, pray to get rid of that mess

WHAT IS LOVE AND HAPPINESS?

There are many different definitions for these words.

The differences in the definitions are one's own.

 In my opinion, everyone can have love & happiness.

I also believe that you can't have one without the other.

This is a fact, for I am a witness.

The highest won't give you more than you can bear.

Some people may say that they know different, meaning they have no faith.

Love and happiness are there for everyone who has faith.

Anyone who doubts my opinion can find a dictionary and

get a definition,

But an authentic and personal explanation is one's own.

WOUNDS

Different things cause wounds

People can even cause wounds

Regardless of what they say, everyone has scars

I wonder if anyone has ever analyzed this before

I do know for a fact that everyone has different wounds

No two wounds are the same

On the contrary, some wounds do run deep like the ones that I harbor

My wounds only surface when I sometimes wake up and wonder

if there is someone that is just as screwed up in the head as me

If there is, do they look like me,

in that I mean are they average looking, disguising their wounds

I look at it like this sometimes, if I am mean to a person

then they might feel an inch of what it is that I am feeling

I do have faith that I won't always have wounds Wounds are like people they come, and they go

I do feel some peace because I recognize that I have wounds

If everyone knew their wounds, then everyone may be able to deal with them in their own time and in their way.

WATER

Water cleans everything.

Water cleans everything from the mind and the body, to the bottom of your soul. Water can wash out stains water can wash away tears, water may even wash out some people's fears, depending on the concern.

What water does for me, is relax me at the end of a hard day

Water cleanses the rough edges of my soul, and the uneasy emotion that I might be feeling.

Some times water prepares me for my day, and what obstacles I may have to overcome, most people don't realize what kind of impact water has on their lives.

Maybe some people may think that my outlook on the water is bullshit and that they only use water to quench their thirst.

Imagine that!

OFFERINGS

That diamond blue sky has so much to offer; all you have to do is lookup. It is reflecting dreams and positive thoughts.

That midnight sky has so much to offer, and the moonlight can be your guide during your late-night walk and talks.

That beach has so much to offer; all you have to do is take a dip. It is ready to cleanse your troubles and offer you peace of mind that no other place can offer.

That park has so much to offer; all you have to do is bring your blanket and music. The grass, butterflies, and laughter will soothe you. It will remind you to appreciate the small things.

Your destiny has so much to offer, never stop traveling your path, we need it, We want it, it is not just yours to keep

but yours to give.

WAKE UP AND SMELL THE PLAN

My definition of fear. Well, it stands for fake evidence appearing real. See negativity will have you feeling discontent and ill will towards another, hold up, that's my definition of envy.

Wake up!

Erase your lower state of consciousness that is controlled either directly or indirectly by the masses or the powers that be.

Please unleash yourself.

Erase your illiteracy,

it's causing you not to be able to process information and therefore not allowing you to express yourself intellectually.

Wake up!

You see, the fact is, some may think its better that you have poor socialization and intellectual skills,

oh and your cognitive ability must be meager along with significant emotional instability.

Wake up!

This place is 90% Fantasy and 10% reality, and these are the ingredients that are instilled in every slave!

INTUITION OR INSECURITY

They say to trust your gut, but does your gut consider your heart and mind?

Is there a meeting, a conference call, what about a simple text message?

Did you see it, can you hear it or do you feel it.

That energy is so strong, so powerful; it can unlock your animal instincts.

Are you talking about those birds and those bees? Are you talking about those butterflies and that lion roar that shakes trees?

But of course. That whisper or that feeling is your ancestors saying don't go that way; that is intuition in it's highest form.

Practice self love, yes, that great love.

There's no need to be insecure, be immune to the options and actions of others. No longer be a victim of endless suffering.

Is it intuition or insecurity? It is both!

Made in the USA
Columbia, SC
23 January 2025

52263131R00019